I0155681

WHY BELIEVING IN JESUS IS A NO-BRAINER

Stop Worrying and Live Forever

LARRY D. KELLEY

HIGH BRIDGE BOOKS
HOUSTON

Why Believing in Jesus Is a No-Brainer
by Larry D. Kelley

Copyright © 2020 by Larry D. Kelley

All rights reserved.

Printed in the United States of America
ISBN (Paperback): 978-1-946615-67-1
ISBN (Hardcover): 978-1-946615-69-5

All rights reserved. Except in the case of brief quotations embodied in critical articles and reviews, no portion of this book may be reproduced, stored in a retrieval system, or transmitted in any form or by any means—electronic, mechanical, photocopy, recording, scanning, or other—without prior written permission from the author.

Scripture quotations marked NASB are from the New American Standard Bible®, Copyright © 1960, 1971, 1977, 1995, 2020 by The Lockman Foundation. All rights reserved.

High Bridge Books titles may be purchased in bulk for educational, business, fundraising, or sales promotional use. For information, please contact High Bridge Books via www.HighBridgeBooks.com/contact.

Published in Houston, Texas by High Bridge Books.

Contents

Preface: Why This Book?

THIS IS A BOOK FOR non-believers, pretenders, and lookers. You know who you are.

You may be someone who feels that they are too cool to believe in Jesus. Or you may be a true skeptic—you really don't see what Jesus can do for you.

You may be one of those people who goes to church once a year. Maybe twice—at Christmas and Easter. Perhaps you feel obligated. Your parents may have made you go to church. Now you have kids and you feel that they deserve that same punishment. It makes for some good stories about grandma and grandpa. Stories about how grandma and grandpa actually lived in a barn when they were kids. They actually took care of farm animals. No, you didn't need an app for that.

You may be one of those lookers. You go to church now and then. You are constantly on the hunt for the right one. No church seems to be an exact fit. You may go for a while and then realize that the congregation is a bunch of hypocrites.

So, you continue to look, thinking that someday you will find the right group that will magically make you a believer in Jesus. But you keep thinking, *If these guys believe in Jesus, I am not sure I should.*

I get it. I have been there. I have gone through all three phases of the program.

Let's face it: Jesus sounds too good to be true. Think of all those miracles. I watch "Penn and Teller's Fool Us." There is always some simple explanation for all those tricks, right?

And it is fun to torment your children by taking them to church the night before Christmas. What five year old wouldn't want to be in church the night before they think they are getting the biggest haul of their life? The look on their little faces is priceless. That isn't really about Jesus. It is a twisted family ritual. You do it because, well, that is the way your family has always done it.

I perfectly understand the association factor. You look at these people who act like "holy rollers" and think, *This is just not my crowd. I may want to learn more about Jesus or even have a casual belief in Jesus, but I am by no means a religious zealot.*

If you are any of these people, this is the book for you. This is an irreverent book about a reverent topic. That's one thing about Jesus—he had a pretty good sense of humor. Although you would never get that from any traditional teaching.

That is the deal. Traditional teaching of the Bible and Jesus can leave a lot to be desired. I can (and actually will) sum up the Bible in a few pages. It really isn't tough. It is a simple story. Frankly, it is the greatest story ever told. Amazing how one book written over thousands of years tells a single story.

Where traditional teaching of the Bible can go off the rails is when you get caught up in the little things and lose sight of the big picture. Even when someone tries to tell you the big picture, they do it in a really boring way.

That is over. In *Why believing in Jesus Is a No-Brainer*, I give you exactly what is in it for you. Trust me, once you understand why, you will become a believer. I promise, it is a very simple process.

You just start believing.

It is such a no-brainer.

Go ahead. Find out why believing in Jesus is a no-brainer.

1

What Is Up with Jesus?!

IF BELIEVING IN JESUS IS such a no-brainer, then why do so many people not believe?

Jesus, the Church, and Christianity have been around a long time. Sometimes, things that have been around for a long time may not feel new, fresh, or relevant.

Perhaps this is a barrier to believing in Jesus. While the message is timeless, not everyone feels it is for today's world. A bigger barrier is that people don't always understand the benefit of believing. And believing in Jesus leads to a huge series of benefits.

Here are three big no-brainer benefits of believing in Jesus.

1. You don't have to worry about screwing up.

2. You get a wingman to help you out.

3. You get to live in eternity.

Believing in Jesus is nearly too good to be true. And maybe that is the biggest barrier of all. It is just too simple.

You believe in Jesus and you get all of this! This is why believing in Jesus is a no-brainer.

I understand the cultural relevance part. Yes, the Bible was written by a number of people without using Microsoft Word. The language can be a bit stilted. The stories can be tedious. And the points can sometimes be obscure.

In this simple book, the key points are provided in plain language. No mumbo jumbo. Straight forward.

Simple.

Believing is the biggest no-brainer out there. Nothing is even close.

2

Don't Worry About Screwing Up

IF YOU BELIEVE IN JESUS, you don't have to worry about screwing up.

The odds are great that we will likely screw up. In fact, sinning is baked into our DNA. We tell a small lie here. We say bad things about someone there. Pretty soon, we have a whole host of sins. Some may be considered small. Some may not. They all add up.

We come from a long, long, long line of sinners. We are talking about dawn-of-time long. When the pastor says that we are all broken, don't take it personally. We are all sinners. And Adam and Eve helped pave the way.

Thanks Adam. Thanks Eve.

Bottom line: Adam and Eve began sinning. We have just followed along.

God gave us the power to choose. Eve made a bad choice. Of course, Adam followed her lead.

Sinning is a crucial part of our makeup.

We might as well come with a "born sinner" label.

On the upside, God is a forgiving God.

In fact, he sent his son, Jesus, to suffer for our sins.

This is one of the greatest gifts of all time.

God has given us free will. He did it in good faith.

He gave us ultimate freedom. It is a part of his idea of perfection.

Maybe God thought, *What is a better gift than the gift of ultimate freedom? You are free to think and act like you want.*

What could go wrong?

Just choose wisely. Yes, there is always a catch to that "freedom" thing.

Who knows where we would be if Adam and Eve had not strayed? What if they fought the baked-in impulse to sin? Can you imagine? It would have set a different tone for humanity.

God told Adam and Eve not to eat from the tree of the knowledge of good and evil.

What happens when you tell someone not to do something? They do it, right?

That is parenting 101. Tell your kid not to do put a marble in his nose. Next time you look, he has a marble up his nose.

Eve got greedy. Eve trusted a snake. This is where "free will" and a lack of judgment collide. After she had eaten the forbidden fruit, she offered it to Adam. Naturally, Adam ate it, too.

Their lack of garden smarts started the sin train.

So, we all have our issues. But it isn't our fault. It is a part of us. We just have to control it.

Having free will is tremendous. It does come with responsibility. If we could exercise good judgment to go along with free will, we would have the greatest combo ever.

You don't have to worry about that. God understands that giving us free will was a key part of making a perfect world. It does have some big downsides. Over time, God tried many ways to enlighten us.

But we are too easily swayed into doing things we shouldn't. We are human.

And it all began with those sorry excuses for snake handlers, Adam and Eve.

The good news is if you follow Jesus, you won't have to worry. Jesus died for our sins. God is a forgiving God.

Not having to worry if you screw up is one of the top reasons believing in Jesus is such a no-brainer.

3

Live Forever—It Beats the Alternative

LIVE FOREVER. THIS IS ONE of the biggest promises in the history of humanity. If you believe in Jesus, you can live forever. We are not talking about living until you look like a wrinkled prune. We are talking about eternal life.

Live forever or don't live forever. Eternal life is the top reason believing in Jesus is such a no-brainer.

Why wouldn't you want to follow him? Because you don't want to live forever?

It feels like our Christian friends just gloss over this. Yet it is spelled out every Sunday.

"May your kingdom come on earth as it is in Heaven."

There it is, Sunday after Sunday. If you are a church goer, you have likely mindlessly repeated those phrases hundreds (if not thousands) of times. Did you ever really stop to think about it?

This is it! It doesn't get any better. All you need to do is believe and follow Jesus and you will live forever. World without end.

Knowing that you have the opportunity to live in whatever form, place, or time that may be seems to be a pretty darn big incentive to follow Jesus.

The chance to live forever sure beats the idea that all there is to life is the small amount of time we have on earth. What have you really got to lose? That's the point.

That is why believing in Jesus is such a no-brainer.

4

Personal Wingman

FATHER. SON. HOLY GHOST. The Holy Trinity.

If you ever attend a church, you are sure to hear about this trio. I don't know about you, but I was always confused by the Holy Ghost or Holy Spirit.

Father is God. Got it. Son is Jesus. Got it. Holy Spirit. Don't got it.

Yet the Holy Spirit is probably one of the best things about believing in God. The Holy Spirit acts as your personal wingman. The Holy Spirit brings you closer to God. The Holy Spirit helps give you goodness.

Talk about the ultimate wingman. It doesn't get any better than God. He helps guide you as you make your way throughout your life.

How many times have you wished you had a really cool wingman to help you out?

This doesn't count the times you are trying to meet someone new at a party. Not a godly look there. Think about having someone who watches you as you work, go to school, or walk down the street. This is an invaluable asset.

You might wonder, *What can this "wingman" really do?*

Having a personal wingman that helps bring you closer to God on a 24/7 basis is a pretty good start.

Having a spiritual wingman is pretty cool. It is a major perk of believing in God.

And it is one more reason believing in Jesus is a no-brainer.

5

Death: God's Ultimate Safeguard

MOST EVERYTHING ON EARTH DIES. Have you ever wondered why?

Yes, scientists discuss DNA and the erosion of the chemical compounds in the body. There may be a much simpler answer.

God put in death as the ultimate safeguard.

Everything was perfect. God was done. He had a great planet. He populated it with a variety of species that are all intertwined. And then he added man and woman.

Then God put in a time limit on everything.

So, death it is.

Death is great. It clears the deck.

It means that no one and no living creature can do harm forever. Can you imagine the havoc that could be wreaked if there was no time limit? Death is a must.

Adam and Eve's son, Cain, killed his brother, Abel. The first family went from disobeying God to really going off the deep end.

Adam and Eve screwed up. Then their offspring really screwed up. What was the world coming to?

That pretty much drove the nail in the coffin, so to speak.

If God had any reservations about imposing the death penalty, Cain crushed them.

Now, can you imagine God's talk with Adam and then Adam's talk with Cain and Seth (the third son)?

"Hey kids, I screwed up. Mom and I listened to a snake. As a result, you guys are screwed up too. Right, Cain? God has put some rules into place to keep things going. That means that I must die. By the way, you will die, too. So, don't get cocky."

There it is. The death safeguard.

While we can't beat the death sentence, we can gain eternal life.

God is a giving God. He puts in the physical guard rails for earth. Then he offers you the opportunity for eternal life.

That is pretty sweet.

Death is great. It is the safeguard so that no one screws things up so bad that it all goes down.

Just another reason believing is a real no-brainer.

6

God Has Your Back

SOMETIMES YOU NEED TO bring in the big gun. Things look bleak. There is no hope.

That seems to be when God steps up and has your back.

Who else would you rather have monitoring your backside? The answer is easy.

Absolutely no one.

God can be the good cop. But he can play bad cop, too. And when he plays bad cop, look out.

Take the case of our man, Moses. God wanted Moses to take his people to Israel. But there was one big problem: the King of Egypt. This king was one of many "wannabe" gods.

The king enslaved Moses and his people.

Typically, being enslaved in those days was the kiss of death. That was the end of the story. But not in this case. God had Moses' back.

Imagine you are the King of Egypt. You have quite a bit of power. Then one day, the water of the Nile River turns to blood. That is not good.

That was God's first shot across the bow. Next, God sent frogs, gnats, flies, disease, hail, and locusts.

God wasn't messing around. This was getting serious.

Just to prove the point that God was (and is) God and the king wasn't, a thick cloud covered Egypt for three days. God finished up with the death of firstborns of both people and animals.

Back in this day, might made right. God took it to him.

The king had enough and released Moses and his people. This was God's deliverance of the Hebrew people from slavery.

This set Moses and his people on a journey to the promised land. Now they were getting somewhere.

But no. It took forty years for Moses to finally get there. Bad GPS? No, it was God teaching Moses and his people many lessons along the way. Sometimes, it just takes time to learn lessons.

Fortunately for Moses and his noble band, God supplied them with manna, a wafer like bread. God also supplied them with plenty of water. He did this for forty years.

God had some real patience. And Moses had some real faith. Moses went through a lot for a small sliver of land.

The real lesson here is that God has your back. Even when things look bleak, he is there. And if he has to play bad cop to solve the problem, he is more than up to the task. Of course, he is more than willing to play good cop if you have the faith.

That is yet another reason believing in Jesus is such a no-brainer.

7

Looks Like I Have to Spell It Out

ONE THING ABOUT GOD IS that he is a straight shooter.

No political double talk. He just lays it out there. Like providing the Ten Commandments.

Even if you are not a Christian, you likely have heard of Moses and the Ten Commandments. God gave the Ten Commandments to his people through Moses at Mount Sinai. These commandments provided the laws for daily living.

Since God didn't have a personal computer, he actually wrote them in stone. That way there would be no misunderstanding.

By this time, well into a thousand or more years of working with humans, God may have thought, *Looks like I am going to have to spell it out for these yahoos. It is not really that hard. Let's spell it out. Just do these ten things.*

God even broke the Ten Commandments into two groups. The first four commandments show how we should work with him. The other six indicate how we should deal with everyone else.

Here they are.

The Ten Commandments

1. Trust God only.

2. Worship God.

3. Use God's name in ways that honor him.

4. Rest on the Sabbath and think about God.

5. Respect and obey your parents.

6. Protect and respect human life.

7. Be true to your husband or wife.

8. Do not take what belongs to others

9. Do not lie about others.

10. Be satisfied with what you have.

God spells out ten simple yet profound rules.

Adam and Eve, it looks like number one has your name all over it. You trusted a snake. You didn't trust God.

And Cain, looks like number six fits you. Killing your brother is not the way to roll. If you look at numbers five through ten, you can find a ton of Bible stories and everyday stories about how people can't do those simple things.

It all began with Adam and Eve. They set the bar really low. And we have kept it there. You would think that over time we might be able to actually check each box on this top ten list. Apparently, practice does not make perfect. We continue to practice the wrong things.

God spent the first few thousand years helping us along. Then he gave us the roadmap. Then he waited another thousand or so years and sent Jesus to show us how to do it.

Just another reason believing in Jesus is a no-brainer.

8

Get Wise

SOME PEOPLE SAY THAT the Bible has nice stories but isn't practical for everyday living. So untrue. Time to wise up.

Solomon, the King of Israel, was one smart guy. He composed over 1,000 songs. He showed great knowledge of the plant and animal world. And he had a vocabulary that was centuries ahead of his time. In fact, there are words in the Bible that only he used.

Solomon was David's son. David was the second king of Israel. David was a shepherd, author, composer, and warrior. Plus, he was king. You may have heard of David and Goliath. This was that David. So Solomon learned from the best. Solomon did have some luxuries, such as a killer palace with a ton of gold. Plus, he was quite the ladies' man. More on that later.

The point is that Solomon actually wrote an entire book on wisdom. The key words in it are "the ability to live life skillfully." You may think this comes from some Tony Robbins book. But no, it comes from Proverbs. You should check it out.

In this book of the Bible, Solomon and some other authors spell out how to relate to God, parents, children, neighbors, and the government.

Proverbs was a follow up to the Ten Commandments. Instead of just giving everyone a ten-point checklist, Proverbs actually spells things out in great detail.

Some people may be thinking that wisdom is just using good judgment. That is true.

Simple things such as obeying your parents or avoiding bad company seem like pretty simple advice. It is. So, why can't we do it?

Wisdom, back in the day, was so much more. The Hebrew idea of wisdom is broader than just using good judgment or knowledge properly.

Wisdom covered all aspects of life.

Wisdom evolved. Shrewdness was a part of wisdom. Too bad it came too late for Adam and Eve.

Another part of wisdom is ethics. This is not only how to treat each other, but how to take care of the planet. Solomon was one of the first environmentalists. He was a deep thinker.

Solomon provides a step-by-step path to wisdom. It is crazy. Management consultants would charge millions of dollars for this stuff. Because the Ten Commandments didn't quite take, Solomon provided both what to do and what not to do. Here are some examples.

Equity

- "A false balance is an abomination to the LORD, but a just weight is His delight" (Prov. 11:1 NASB). Solomon is talking about being equitable. Something we don't always see today.

Humility

- "When pride comes, then comes dishonor, But with the humble is wisdom" (Prov. 11:2

NASB). Simple statement. Stay
humble.

Integrity

- "The integrity of the upright
  will guide them, But the crook-
  edness of the treacherous will
  destroy them" (Prov. 11:3
  NASB). Again, this guy was
  spot on.

Discipline

- "Whoever loves discipline
  loves knowledge, But he who
  hates reproof is stupid" (Prov.
  12:1 NASB). They didn't sugar-
  coat it back then.

Generosity

- "He who withholds grain, the
  people will curse him, But
  blessing will be on the head of
  him who sells it" (Prov. 11:26
  NASB). You don't want to be
  cursed.

These five examples are just the start from a book that contains 30 chapters and roughly 25 wisdom nuggets per chapter. It offers over 700 ways to better your life. Just pick a few and do them. Each wisdom nugget is spelled out in great detail by the wise one himself, Solomon.

As Solomon says, "Do not be lazy." Lazy men get no food. In this case, the food is more than a Big Mac. It is the wisdom of life.

So, wise up. Check it out.

Just another reason believing is a no-brainer.

9

One Love

THE BIBLE IS FILLED WITH tons of great stuff. Wisdom. Inspiration. Plus timeless moral lessons.

You may not know that King Solomon was also the love doctor. Yes, he was the original Barry White. In fact, like Barry White, the Love Walrus, Solomon wrote one of the all-time best love songs. It is called the "song of songs" and "the best song," and in the Bible, it is entitled The Song of Solomon.

Lots of folks write love songs. Do they really know anything about love? Solomon, the love doctor, certainly did. According to the Bible, about the time Solomon wrote his love song, he had accumulated 60 queens and 80 concubines. Wow. So, Solomon was married to 60 women and had another 80 on the side. One thing's for certain: this guy knows something about women.

Solomon's harem reportedly reached 700 queens and 300 concubines. That is one thousand women. It has to be some sort of record. If this guy was on Tinder, he would always be swiping right.

So when Solomon writes about courtship, love, and marriage, he has been around the block a few times. He knows what he is talking about. One lesson he learned was that more is not always a good thing.

The cool thing about Solomon's song is that after all these women, Solomon figured out that love is a special thing. The song he wrote was about a special lady that Solomon fell in love with.

He spurned the other one thousand for this one.

His song is about a true love. A singular love. One that can't be fulfilled by the countless others. He details it all in his song. He really has some good love advice.

Solomon had a way with words. He was better than Cyrano de Bergerac. Just check out some of these pearls.

- "Your lips, my bride, drip with honey."

- "Your eyes are like doves behind your veil."

- "The curves of your hips are like jewels."

- "You are a garden spring."

- "Your love is like the best wine."

No wonder Solomon was a ladies' man. He had romance oozing out of his pores. He had some timeless tips on love. The song is how he moved from romance to marriage to love. It is a beautiful thing.

Of course, Solomon's "love story" has an important moral. The first is to love your wife, not *wives*. The second is to love God. Solomon was one wise man.

And this is just another reason believing is a no-brainer.

10

The Do-Over

SOMETIMES, PEOPLE THINK that you have to be a "Puritan" to believe in Jesus. Since most of us have done bad things, there can be a belief that it is too late to be saved. We have blown our shot at anything resembling a good life and don't even want to think about an afterlife.

But it is never too late. You still have a chance. You have to take some action but the payoff is pretty sweet.

You may think that the story of Jonah and the giant fish is just about a fish who ate Jonah. But it is much more. It is the classic story of "The Do-Over."

Even though Jonah was a big prophet, Jonah could be a real jerk. God asked Jonah to help him out. He wanted Jonah to set some people straight in a town filled with sinners. This town was a big rival to Jonah's town.

You would think that Jonah would be honored by this request. But no—Jonah wouldn't do it. Jonah must have felt like he was being asked to help the visiting team. In fact, Jonah was so adamant not to help God with this request that he said that he would rather die than to do the deed. Jonah then walked away from God.

God heard this response ("I would rather die") and possibly thought, *I can arrange that.*

So he did.

Jonah was on a boat. Suddenly, he was cast overboard. Then a giant fish swallowed him. Now, this is where the story gets interesting. Jonah went to Sheol, which is a place of darkness where the dead are sent. Yep, you heard it here. Jonah was with the dead. He has gone to the underworld.

The place of the dead is not a great place to be.

This finally got Jonah's attention. So, as a last gasp, Jonah asked for God's forgiveness. Jonah was now willing to do whatever God wanted him to do. Funny how that seems to work when you have really screwed things up.

On the third day, God raised Jonah from the dead. The giant fish turned out to be the savior of Jonah after all.

Jonah had one of the greatest do-overs of all time. Jonah was in a dark place. Yet he was brought back to life to do some good. He was down and out, yet he got a second chance.

Whatever you have done, odds are that you are not actually in the place of the dead.

Everyone needs a second chance. Even those who have done enough to be banished to the underworld.

You can get a second chance to turn your life around. There is a pretty sweet afterlife waiting for you if you do.

It sure beats waiting in the stinky belly of a big fish.

And this is just another reason to believe in Jesus.

11

It Does Take Faith

FAITH SOMETIMES TAKES, well, a leap of faith. Just believe.

I remember a kid we made fun of for always dressing up to go to school. This kid was wearing a suit when he was ten years old. He even had a little briefcase.

What a dork!

Every day, this kid came to school in a suit. Very polite.

Teachers loved him. Everyone else hated him. Why? Because he was different. He wore that suit because he said that, someday, he was going to be in the theater. And he always wanted to look his best. He was in an ongoing audition.

He parlayed that suit into roles in the high school play, into a scholarship to Julliard, and into ongoing roles on Broadway.

Had we known that, we all would have worn suits, too.

The point of this story is that you have to have faith. The kid believed. And it served him well. All those years of ridicule were nothing since he accomplished his goal.

Now, imagine that you are Noah. You know, the guy with the ark. Yes, that Noah.

Talk about ridicule. God told Noah to build an ARK.

"Why?" asked Noah.

"Trust me," said God.

So, Noah trusted God. He had faith. And it wasn't easy. People made fun of him. His family was totally embarrassed. Those poor kids of Noah. They had to be beside themselves. Every kid on the planet and their parents thought Noah was crazy.

Yet Noah continued.

Little did Noah know what God had in mind. God had tried a lot of different ways to get us to believe in him. Sometimes, he was good cop, helping people out. Sometimes, he was bad cop, pounding those who were out of line.

He may have thought, *Noah—here is a guy who believes in me. I can trust him no matter what. I am going to clear the deck. Noah and his family go forward, plus the animals.*

Everyone else—out of the boat.

That was it. The point is that sometimes you have to have faith. It may require taking some flak. In the end, it will be worth it.

Being on the boat is the place to be.

This is yet another reason believing is a no-brainer.

12

The Time Is Right

THE OLD TESTAMENT OF the Bible was largely the buildup to Jesus. In the Old Testament, many prophets forecast that Jesus would come.

Now, these prophets predicted this for thousands of years. This is like the little kid in the car on a family road trip asking, "Are we there yet? Are we there yet? Are we there yet?"

After a while, you become skeptical. When asked about the timing of Jesus, the prophets would say, "When the time is right." Great. Another non-answer. This went on for thousands of years. The kids ask, "Are we there yet?" And the prophets say, "He will arrive when the time is right."

So, the question is, "When is the time right?"

The timing of Jesus was so incredible that this alone was reason enough that believing in Jesus is a no-brainer.

Jesus could have arrived at any time in history. He would be the Son of God. The timing of Jesus was perfect.

Let me give you one name. Caesar. Julius Augustus Caesar. That is three. Caesar ruled about forty years before Jesus arrived on the scene. Caesar fancied himself a god. He made everyone act like he was a god. He took out those who didn't go along. Not a nice guy.

The Roman Empire was getting a bit too big for its britches. And the guys who ruled at various times were nut cases. Caesar—maniac. Nero—crazy. Caligula—demented.

And we could go on and on.

These were bad dudes. And they were super posers. God posers. And if you think back to the Ten Commandments, one of those said not to worship false Gods. Looks like we have a winner here.

As the real God watched this Roman insanity unfold, he must have thought, *Now it's time!*

It was time to send in Jesus. He had work to do. Given the Roman orgies of the time, he had plenty of sins to clean up.

Rome was a sinner's paradise. But only if you were the top dog. Otherwise, things were not too good for you.

King Herod, the Rome-appointed ruler of Judea at the time of Jesus, was no prize either. He was as maniacal as any of these other rulers.

This is the context that Jesus stepped into.

This is why the timing of Jesus was so perfect. And guess what? The rise of Jesus led to the demise of all those Roman shenanigans.

The timing couldn't have been better. Consider the contrast between Roman and royal posers as gods and the son of the real God. Pretty stark difference.

And that is one of the big reasons believing in Jesus is such a no-brainer.

13

Mary & Joseph: Jesus' Fearless Parents

MARY AND JOSEPH, JESUS' parents, were fearless. Their story shows that you can do things well beyond what you think. You just have to believe.

Let's take Mary. God sent one of his angel buddies to see if she would be willing to conceive Jesus. If some "being" asks you that, it just might freak you out. It does seem like a lot to ask.

Mary was cool about it. She wasn't freaked. In fact, she was honored that she was chosen. What a great attitude.

Now, being a single mom in those days was not highly thought of. In fact, there could be serious consequences for having a child out of wedlock.

That is where Joseph comes into the picture. Old Joe had to take Mary and baby into his household. Now this was also a big ask, especially since he wasn't involved in her pregnancy.

Poor Joe; as a lawyer might say, he could neither confirm nor deny that the baby was his. He had to play along. That was the pact that he made. He must have taken a lot of crap.

Mary likely took a lot of crap, too.

"Of all the guys in town, you picked that dude? C'mon, you can do better."

Mary surely caught more than her share of sideways glances and stares.

And lots of mumbling and whispering behind the back.

It was likely a long nine months.

That is why you have to hand it to the parents of Jesus. They could have broken down.

They were likely dying to tell people about what was about to unfold. They held it together.

If that isn't enough, how about raising the Son of God? That can't be easy. Talk about a huge responsibility. They had to take care of this kid until he could save the world.

Are you kidding me?

Let's start at a beginning.

Mary had the baby in a barn. This sounds romantic, surrounded by farm animals and lying in the straw; but birthing a baby isn't easy. Can you imagine doing something like that today?

Then the three wise men came for a visit, bringing gifts for the baby. As a parent, strangers bringing gifts to a baby seems a little weird, doesn't it? Who were these guys?

Once they knew why they were there, the pressure must have been incredible. They recognized that Jesus was the savior of the world. Yet he was just a baby. He was as vulnerable as any other child. Big problem.

To complicate matters, the king at the time was none too pleased. He heard that a child of God had been born. So he sent his goon squad out to kill the baby. In the process, the goons basically ended up killing just about any kid under the age of two. Brutal.

So Mary and Joseph were on the run with the most important child of all time. Thank goodness God had their back. They needed it.

Somehow, they got past this initial onslaught. Then they had to raise the child. Talk about more pressure. Raising a kid is no easy task under any circumstances. But raising God's only child—talk about huge pressure.

They couldn't really let on that the kid was special. Yet they knew he was special. So the balancing act began. To make this even tougher, as Jesus grew up, he began to learn that he had some pretty special powers.

There is not a ton written about Jesus growing up. But there are a few books that never made it into the Bible that talk about Jesus learning about his vast array of powers. There are stories of Jesus bringing a dead bird to life. Can you imagine the parent's discussion with Jesus over this?

"Jesus, I know you want to save everything, but you are going to have to let it go."

It is scary. Imagine a kid with a super powers. That was Jesus. He had amazing power and was still a kid. And he could be a handful. Here is an example.

When Jesus was 12, he went to the Temple without his parent's permission and questioned some of the clergy there about the ways of the Lord. The clergy had their minds blown. Who was this kid? And how did he know so much about the Bible?

While this sounds innocent enough, just remember that the powers that be at the time didn't want Jesus horning in on their action. News can travel fast. The last thing you want is someone chatting about some kid who seems like a Bible savant. Maybe Joseph had to diffuse the situation with some story that a roving clergy did some intensive Bible training in their village.

Somehow, through his early years, Jesus managed to stay out of sight of the powers that be. Perhaps they assumed that the goon squad nabbed him long ago.

Mary and Joseph decided that it wasn't enough pressure, so they had some kids on their own. They really were gluttons for punishment.

James was Jesus' brother. Talk about big shoes to fill. Growing up in Jesus' shadow was likely not easy. And think of how they would have to parent a regular child when they already had the "chosen one" in their house.

"Why can't I walk on water? Why can't I bring things back to life?"

What did they say to James when he asked those types of questions? You know how little kids are. They ask all sorts of embarrassing questions.

Give props to Mary and Joseph. They have to be considered for the parents' hall of fame. They rose to extraordinary lengths to prep Jesus for saving humanity.

That is one heck of a resume. Normal people can do extraordinary things.

Just one more reason it is such a no-brainer to believe in Jesus.

14

Champion for the Underdog

DO YOU REMEMBER WHEN your complexion was a pepperoni pizza? Maybe you couldn't keep a job. Or perhaps you were a little too into sex, drugs, and rock and roll.

Welcome aboard the Jesus misfit train. Jesus was the champion of the underdog.

And his group of misfits was not just a gritty story that makes your heart bleed. We are talking about folks like lepers, tax collectors, prostitutes, and general down and outers.

You think your complexion was bad. Have you ever seen a leper? Yeow. Leprosy or Hansen's disease, as it is now called, is serious. While it still exists today, it is now treatable. It wasn't back in the day. So lepers were considered outcasts. A leper didn't have to have leprosy to be considered a leper. Throw in some bad skin or a few blemishes and you were a leper. You were pretty much banished faster than the first bachelor on The Bachelorette.

Tax collectors were no prize either. Everyone hated them. Tax collectors made the Romans' lives easier and Jews' lives harder. They worked hard for their money and this guy came and took it. What?!

Tax collectors weren't winning any popularity contests.

Prostitution has been around since 2400 BC. Amazing, when you think about it. Like tax collectors, prostitutes served the Romans. The money for their service came from taxes. Not exactly the way anyone would want their tax dollars spent. As with tax collectors, prostitutes were reviled.

God gave Moses the Ten Commandments and it seemed like there was an illegal or naughty industry that sprung up around each one.

No wonder we can't get anywhere in our society.

Basically, Jesus said to the down and outers, "What do you have to lose? Believe in me and you will be redeemed."

When you know that you are an outcast, why not see if you can get in with the "in" crowd? Jesus took anyone and everyone in. You really have to admire the guy.

No matter who you were, Jesus invited you in.

Sometimes people are a bit leery of this philosophy. It is that "I am not sure I want to be in a club that lets me in" mentality. Perfectly understandable. No exclusivity.

The trick to joining this club was to first believe in Jesus. Ok, that wasn't super tough.

The beauty of believing in Jesus is that no matter who you are, you are eligible to join the club.

Just another reason to believe in Jesus.

15

The Man.
The Miracles.

WE ALL KNOW THAT JESUS was *the man*. Many know Jesus by his miracles. He walked on water. He turned water into wine. He got fish out of the water. Anything with water, he had it.

What most people don't realize is how many miracles Jesus performed.

He wasn't just a one-hit wonder. He performed miracle after miracle. In fact, the Bible cites about 37 different miracles. And those are just the ones that were documented. Who knows how many more he performed? Here is a sampling of his greatest hits.

- Got an ailment? No problem. Jesus was a healing machine. He healed lepers, paralytics, the blind, the deaf, the disabled, and the infirm.

- Need some food? No problem. Jesus fed four thousand folks and then fed another five thousand. We are talking about thousands of people. And he was pretty good at catching fish. No need for a hook. He just commands them to come.

- Need more proof? No problem. Let's walk on water. That sounds fun. Or let's turn water into wine. Another party pleaser. Jesus did have a playful side to him.

- Naturally, the coup de grace is rising from the dead.

Even with all these miracles, the more impressive are the miracles he didn't do. Let's face it—Jesus had superpowers. He certainly could have escaped from the Roman soldiers.

He could have wiped out the king. But he didn't.

Jesus really didn't use his superpowers until he was in his 30s. That means that he spent the first 30 years of his life being a "regular guy." That is like asking Clark Kent not to be Superman. Just be happy doing those news stories, Clark. Don't do anything else.

Performing miracles can be a double-edged sword. Jesus knew he had to demonstrate otherworldly powers to convince the masses that he was not just another guy. After the 37th miracle, they likely got the message that Jesus was the "real deal."

The bad news was that he was on the radar screen. And he was threatening to a number of people in power. The clerics at the time wove a narrative that he was the devil. How else could someone do these things? He was battling some bad press from them.

Of course, the king and all of the folks in power were none too pleased. This was a man with some legit power. When you want the people to think you are a god, you don't want any competition from the real God.

The miracles of Jesus provided proof that Jesus was real. Some of the miracles were performed in private. But there were plenty of miracles witnessed by a number of people, so there was no question that they didn't happen.

Jesus had a lot of tools on his tool belt. He used miracles to lay a base of social proof that he was the son of God.

This is just another reason believing in Jesus is a no-brainer.

16

The Fab Four

IF YOU ARE A BABY BOOMER, when you see the phrase "the fab four," your mind may go to the Beatles. Back in the 1960s, those four Brits with the shaggy hair dominated the music scene like no other group. It was crazy. They were Elvis times four. The world was not the same.

That brings me to the "original fab four": Matthew, Mark, Luke, and John.

The world was never the same after they told the world about Jesus. These four were the key figures in spreading the word of God. Without them, Jesus may have been a nice footnote in history. Jesus made things real. The fab four helped make Jesus' teachings into an ongoing movement.

Amazing that about a third of the planet believes in Jesus. Millions of people believe. During the time of the fab four, there was no internet, no social media. Not even a community newspaper. Nada. So for these guys to get things rolling and keep them rolling was truly amazing.

The other big thing that the fab four did was give four different perspectives on the life and teaching of Jesus. They captured different aspects of his life and wrote to different audiences. See, even back in the day, the fab four understood the power of communication. Jews, Gentiles, and Romans all took away something a bit different from the Jesus experience. And the fab four knew this and addressed their needs in the four gospels.

Matthew wrote about Jesus' strength and royal authority. Mark wrote about Jesus' strength and power. Luke, who wrote the history of Jesus, had a theme of wisdom and character. John focused on the theological meaning of Jesus' actions and emphasized who Jesus was rather than what he did.

John, batting cleanup for the fab four, sums it up with this: "you may believe that Jesus is the Christ, the Son of God; and that believing you may have life in His name" (John 20:31 NASB).

That is the headline. Believe in Jesus and you have the promise of eternal life. It doesn't get much bigger than that. That was powerful back then. It led to the biggest social movement in the earth's history. One can only wonder what would happen if Jesus had been alive today in the world of instant communication. The fab four put Jesus' teachings into motion.

This is just one more reason believing in Jesus is such a no-brainier.

17

Just Act

HYPOCRITES ARE EVERYWHERE. Lots of them run for public office. They talk a good game. But they don't walk the walk. The same can be said for many church goers. They put on a good act, but they don't actually act. They don't put their faith into action.

It is a valid point. One who did talk the talk and walk the walk was Paul. Paul of the Bible. Paul the apostle. Paul who wrote the book of Romans.

Paul was the most eloquent and persuasive teacher of the Bible (of course, after Jesus). He was born a Jew, a Roman citizen, and a Pharisee. Basically, Paul went the wrong way for many years, persecuting Christians until he met Jesus.

Talk about a life turned around. Paul became the central figure in doing mission work. Paul had seen it all. He persecuted

Christians. Then he became one and was persecuted himself. He did some time in prison. He was flogged. And yet he hung in there.

The key to Paul was that he did something. He acted. He took many huge mission trips, including going to Asia to spread the good word. But his mission trips would not have been possible except for the handiwork of the Roman Empire.

Romans were building fools. Beyond building arenas and temples, they built tons of roads. Perfect timing. Those roads allowed Paul to help spread the word.

Being a Roman citizen meant that Paul had privileges in Rome. His letters to Rome outlined the tenets of Jesus' teachings. While the religious elite of Rome may not have liked it, there were those who respected Paul. And that helped pave the way (pun intended) for Paul to be one of the key figures in the early church.

Beyond his letter to Rome (i.e. Romans), Paul also wrote much of the New Testament. If there was a town that needed some counseling, Paul sent them a letter.

He was a letter-writing machine. He was bound and determined to get the message out. You have to admire his action.

Speaking of taking action, the book of Acts lays out what we need to do to support Jesus. Acts sums up what we need to do to grow the church. Beyond that, it was a quick tutorial on how to live and make others' lives better. It encourages us to act.

Paul was a man of action. He put a mega horn to Jesus' message. Paul showed us the way. Act. Not just an act.

This is just one more reason believing in Jesus is a no-brainer.

18

Self-Help Guru

THE SELF-HELP INDUSTRY in the US generates upwards of $10 billion. People need help. People want help. And people are spending big bucks on books, seminars, and consultants to gain enlightenment.

You don't need to spend big bucks seeking enlightenment. We have covered that Jesus was likely the biggest self-help guru to ever grace the planet. And the Bible is the best self-help book on the market.

What you may not know is how Paul was the original self-help management guru.

Yes, that same Paul who was an apostle and wrote the majority of the New Testament. Between his mission work and writing, Paul cranked out a couple of epistles (a funny word for a letter) to Timothy and Titus.

These two guys were facing management challenges. Both were floundering in their first management job. They were sent to two churches to do a "turnaround job." That is management speak for fixing a big organizational problem.

In both cases, Timothy and Titus were replacing more experienced guys. Both were charged with changing the culture and building a new leadership team.

Paul, from prison, mind you, counseled Timothy and Titus on what to do and how to do it. It was a crash course in management from the master. The reason this management challenge was so important was that Paul was old and in a Roman prison, and he knew he needed some younger folks to take charge and maintain his momentum.

Paul laid out how to set up a culture by providing what qualifications were needed for a bishop in the church. He gave a short course on being a leader. Then he provided instruction on how to teach, tithe, and treat all people, with special emphasis on widows, elders, and slaves.

In fact, you can organize Paul's management book into organization, operations, obedience, and offenders. He provides the management textbook of how to organize, how to set up the proper operation structure, how to work within the operation, and what to watch out for that will hurt the organization.

It is a classic. It can apply to just about any business today. And the good news was that it worked. The two Ts, Timothy and Titus, went on the change their churches and continued to spread the word long after Paul died.

Just as a quick point, each of these letters are just a few pages in length. They are the best and briefest management tips available on the market today. So save your money. Help yourself.

This is just another reason believing in Jesus is a no-brainer.

19

Woman Power

EMPOWERING WOMEN. Not something typically associated with the Bible. Yet, Jesus was definitely one of the early advocates for women. Women played a key role in his ascent—both literally and figuratively.

Mary, Jesus' mom, was obviously the key woman. No Mary, no Jesus. And Mary was more than just a celebrity mother. Mary, as we have talked about, was one super strong woman, both mentally and physically. You would expect nothing less from the mother of Christ.

Mary Magdalene, a running buddy of Jesus, was also a central figure in Jesus' time.

Mary M. was a key person at Jesus' tomb. And she was the first person that Jesus talked to after he arose from the grave.

So, the Marys were key parts of Jesus being Jesus. Jesus recognized women and made them a key part of the program.

The Bible also features a woman long before Jesus who must be one of the first women to lean in.

Her name was Deborah.

Deborah lived more than a thousand years before Jesus. She set people straight about the role women can play in society.

Deborah was a serious trailblazer.

Deborah was the first (and possibly only) female judge for thousands of years. The Bible mentions only one woman who became a judge: Deborah.

Deborah lived about 3,000-4,000 years ago, long before the women's suffrage movement.

People talk about the business world being a "boys club" now. Can you imagine what it was like way before Christ? That had to have been one serious boys club.

No women allowed.

Yet somehow, Deborah had the guts to take on the boys. She became a judge.

And that wasn't even the half of it. Deborah was a judge, a prophet, and a military strategist.

Not a bad resume, eh?

Deborah helped inspire the Israelites to a victory over their oppressors who were living in the promised land. She was the military strategy lead on this conquest. In fact, the "general," Barak, wouldn't go into battle without her and gave her all the credit for the victory. Deborah was such a rock star that she has her own song dedicated to her battle.

Deborah was a huge forerunner to showing the way for women in society. Jesus then opened the floodgates.

This is just another reason believing in Jesus is such a no-brainer.

20

Eat, Drink, and Be Merry

DO YOU LIKE TO EAT? Maybe have a drink? Or just have fun? Welcome to Christianity. The whole religion is a big celebration.

And you guessed right—it is just one more reason to believe in Jesus.

Christmas isn't Christmas without Christ.

I realize that Coca-Cola, Macy's, and others have made it into a huge commercial endeavor. Marketing is a beautiful thing, but it is not the reason for the celebration.

Many associate Christmas with general gift giving and stories about Santa and his reindeer.

The bottom line is that Christmas wouldn't be Christmas without Jesus Christ.

What would you rather celebrate—getting a sweater that you won't wear or having all your sins forgiven?

Easter is the most important celebration. No, it isn't just a big chocolate egg hunt designed by Hershey's to pump up sales after Halloween. It is to celebrate the rise of Jesus from the grave. Do you remember that "world without end" that we talked about? This is it. This is the celebration of the resurrection of Christ.

Thanksgiving is another celebration of the year. It is more than stuffing your face with turkey and yams and then watching football in a catatonic state. All that is true, but Thanksgiving is giving thanks for a great harvest. And who are we giving thanks to? That's right. Jesus, of course.

If you are Jewish, the feasts don't stop here. There are many Jewish celebrations, such as the Three Pilgrimage Festivals, Pesach (Passover), Shavuot, and the weeks leading into Pentecost and Sukkot, when ancient Jews made the pilgrimage to Israel. And of course, there is Hanukah.

If you are a foodie, you can really get into Jewish feast culture. The Feast of Booths commemorates the wandering in the wilderness before finding the promised land. The Feast of Purim or the Feast of Lots celebrates the deliverance of Jews from the schemes of Hamas. The Feast of Trumpets has no reason other than people like to eat and blow a trumpet.

We are talking about a lot of feasts. The people like to celebrate and eat. Now that is a religion everyone can get behind.

The world would be a pretty dull place without Jesus. The biggest parties of the year are based on celebrating him. Don't you feel just a little bit hypocritical celebrating without really believing?

Believing in Jesus lets you to eat, drink, and be merry to celebrate the Son of God. Cheers.

Just another great reason to believe in Jesus.

21

It's Worth the Pain

IF YOU PLAYED SPORTS, you likely "played through the pain" at some point in your athletic career. Maybe it wasn't as dramatic as 1995 Olympic gymnast, Kerri Strug of the USA, who broke her ankle and then nailed a vault on one leg to win a Gold. Now that was dramatic.

The sports world is full of many memorable moments when players played with broken bones, torn muscles, or in total exhaustion. Why endure the pain? Some call it gritty. Others call it crazy. All of these athletes had one thing in common: they believed in a common purpose. The purpose is usually bigger than themselves. Perhaps it's to help the team win the game. That purpose is worth the pain.

Having a strong purpose is the key to overcoming a lot of obstacles. Think about another type of pain—the pain of being persecuted. There isn't a religion that hasn't had its share of persecution. It comes with the territory.

This is especially true when you do something new—like bringing Christianity to the world. All those early apostles were persecuted. Paul was in and out of prison so much that people thought he was a serial criminal. He persevered. The reason? He had a purpose. And it was much bigger than himself.

Most things worth doing come with some pain. Ladies, you can blame Eve for that child birth pain. Her dalliance with that snake cost you some grief. But having kids is worth the pain. That is a higher purpose.

This was one reason Jesus suffered for us. He wanted to show us that the pain was real, but also demonstrate that it was worth it to have the purpose fulfilled.

So when you think you don't have enough energy, things are really tough, or those mean people are too much, just think about the purpose on your path. That will help you push through the pain. Sometimes, believing will be painful. Accept it. Pain can lead to growth. Furthering Jesus' mission is worth the pain.

This is just another reason believing in Jesus is a no-brainer.

22

Find Your Purpose

IF YOU ARE LIKE MOST people, you go through life just making do. You may have a job. You may have a family. You may own a home. Or you may not have anything at all. Sometimes, it is difficult to find a purpose.

You get up. You go to work. You come home. You help your son with his homework. You walk the dog. You watch television. You go to sleep. And you do it all over again. And you may do this day after day.

No wonder a lot of us wonder, *Is this really all there is to life? Isn't there something more?*

That is where believing in Jesus comes in. If you believe in Jesus and put that faith into action, you have a purpose in life. And that purpose that will pay off in the afterlife. You can't beat that.

You are but a speck in time between the past and the future. Your years on earth don't add up to more than a blip in history. So make the most of it.

Step back. Think about what your job should be on this planet. Is it to raise a family? Teach others? Help others? Pick up after others?

It doesn't have to be some grand career. In fact, sometimes the simplest jobs may be the best ways to serve Jesus. And that is your ultimate purpose in life.

It is simple. Serve Jesus. Little things add up. If you go into each day with the idea that you will find a way to serve Jesus, you will do just fine.

Once you have a purpose, you should be motivated to make it happen. What is it that needs doing that you know something about and likely won't happen if you don't do it? That is a great place to start.

Finding your purpose is another reason believing in Jesus is a no-brainer.

23

The Second Coming

EVERYONE LOVES AN encore performance. Raise that lighter overhead. Scream. Clap. And hope that they come back on stage to do another song. Who doesn't want more?

More episodes, more songs, more books, more videos. Give me MORE! We want more!

If you like Jesus, the first act, there is the promise of a second act. That is how the Bible ends. It ends with a promise that Jesus will return. And who wouldn't want to see that? Talk about a once in a lifetime event.

Now, it took some time for Jesus to get here for Act One. The prophets promised it for thousands of years. So, it could be a while before we see Act Two. As we saw in Act One, the wait was worth it.

He came at the perfect time for Act One. The world needed him. Rome needed to be knocked down a peg or two. And the movement needed to happen.

So the movement has happened. And about a third of the planet is on board.

That means that two thirds aren't on board. There is unfinished business to attend to.

You might notice that the world isn't perfect.

Jesus came to show us the way. Do we always follow his lessons? You tell me.

Now that isn't to say that everything is in the dumpster. Some people are trying to make things better. On the other hand, there are people are trying to make things better just for them. Therein lies the problem.

When will he come? Perhaps any day now. We have to be patient. He will know when the time is right. Another act. An encore presentation. Isn't it great to know that there will be a second coming?

This is just another reason believing in Jesus is a no-brainer.

24

Yes, It Is a No-Brainer

THIS BOOK IS BASED ON the fact that believing in Jesus is a real no-brainer.

A no-brainer is where there a clear and obvious right decision or choice is made easily, requiring no real thought to decide what to do.

It is obvious. It is clear. It is a true no-brainer. Let's take a look at a couple of examples.

- If someone offered you a million dollars free and clear with no strings attached, would you consider that a no-brainer? Of course.

- If your doctor told you that taking one pill would protect you from all disease, would you take it? Naturally.

Believing in Jesus is even more obvious than either of these examples. Let's review. Your sins will be forgiven. You get a wingman to bring you closer to God. Oh, and you will live in eternity. Now, does that sound like a no-brainer?

And there are even more benefits that are outlined in this book. It is obvious. It is clear. It is a true no-brainer.

Believing in Jesus is a *no-brainer*.

Today is a great day to start. Believe.

25

Bible Brief Bonus

THE STANDARD BIBLE has around 1200 pages. There are tons of nuggets of wisdom found in each book of the Bible. While the Bible is large, the overall story is amazingly simple. The Bible is a story about redemption.

The following is your Bible brief.

1. God creates the universe.

2. God creates man/woman.

3. Man/woman disobey God.

4. God tries to prop up man/woman.

5. God sends in his son, Jesus.

6. Jesus shows the way. The movement begins.

7. Jesus dies for our sins.

8. On the third day Jesus is res-
    urrected.

9. The Apostles spread the
    movement.

10. Jesus promises to come again.
    TBD.

That is the basic story.

Naturally, there is a lot of detail to fill in. The Bible is filled with an incredible number of stories, lessons, and words to live by. Please check it out.

Thanks for reading.

Keep on believing.

About the Author

Larry D. Kelley is an author, educator, and strategic communication professional.

Larry is a professor of advertising. He has authored ten textbooks on advertising that have been adopted at hundreds of colleges and universities.

Prior to moving into academia, Larry was an executive at a number of large advertising firms where he was involved in strategic planning for a wide range of brands.

This book was inspired by the need to help others see the compelling benefits for believing in Jesus.

Hence, the idea of the "no-brainer" was born. As was the idea to make a book about religion simple, fun, and accessible.

Thanks for reading. I hope you enjoy it.

www.ingramcontent.com/pod-product-compliance
Lightning Source LLC
LaVergne TN
LVHW041324080426
835513LV00008B/583